The deep thoughts and ponderings of:

"Fill your paper with the breathings of your heart."

—William Wordsworth

FEATURING THE DESIGNS OF BEN KWOK

You just got exciting news!
Who's the first person you tell? Why?

You run into your time-travelling future self.
What do you ask yourself?

_____

_____

_____

_____

_____

_____

_____

_____

_____

_____

_____

_____

_____

_____

_____

_____

_____

_____

_____

_____

_____

What was your most successful New Year's resolution?

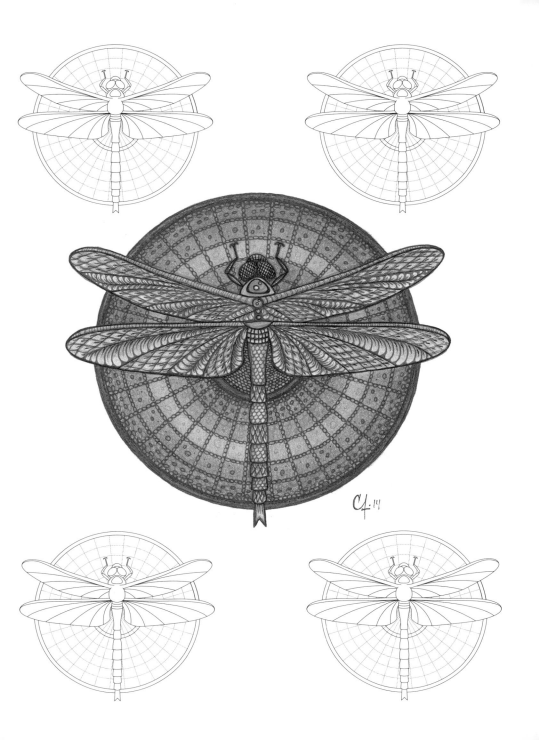

What have you worked the hardest for?

How do you cheer yourself up?

Love or money?

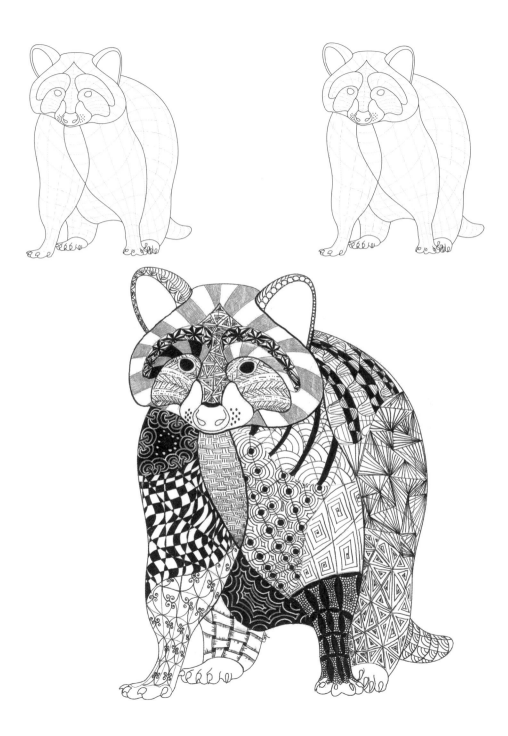

What have you stopped yourself from buying recently?

You have an unexpectedly free day. What do you do?

_____

_____

_____

_____

_____

_____

_____

_____

_____

_____

_____

_____

_____

_____

_____

_____

_____

_____

_____

_____

_____

_____

What was the best meal you've ever had?

Whom are you grateful for?
When was the last time you talked to them?

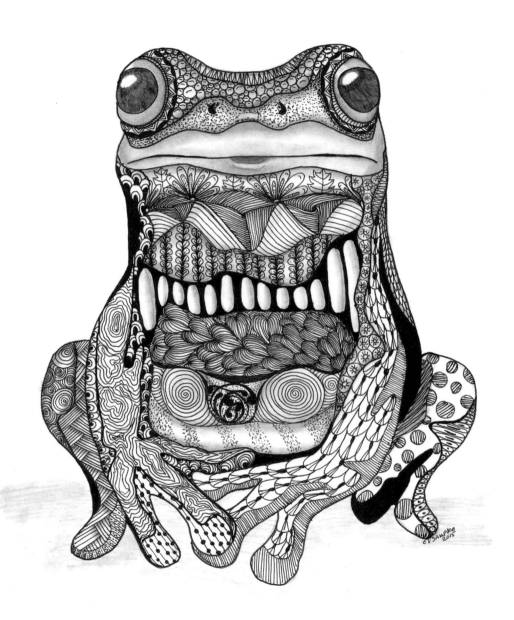

What are three things you can see right now that you like?

What is your go-to activity when you want to procrastinate?

Dogs or cats?

What was the last compliment you gave someone? How was it received?

What color is your mood today?

When was the last time you cried? Why?

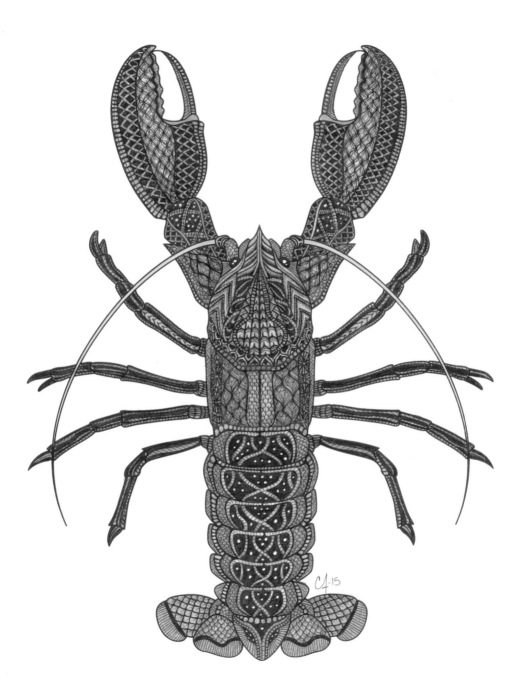

What did you want to be when you grew up? Did you change your mind along the way?

How would your best friend describe you? Your mother? Your pet?

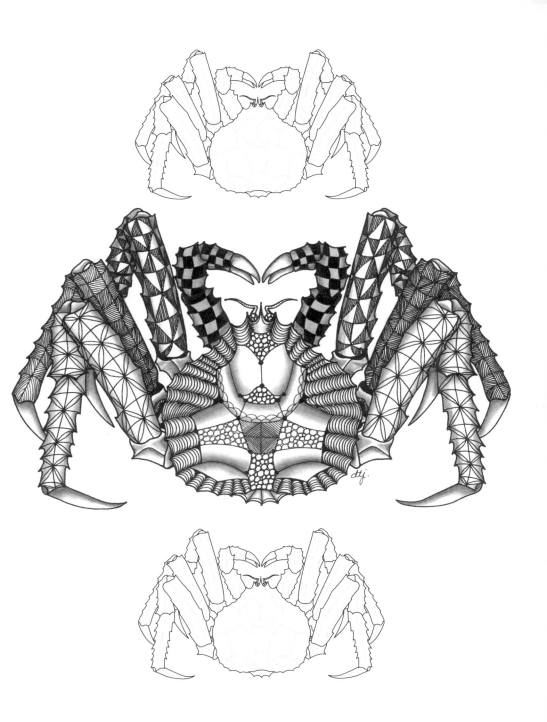

You find a magic lamp, and the genie inside offers to change one thing in your life. What do you choose?

_____

_____

_____

_____

_____

_____

_____

_____

_____

_____

_____

_____

_____

_____

_____

_____

_____

_____

_____

_____

_____

What kind of friend are you?

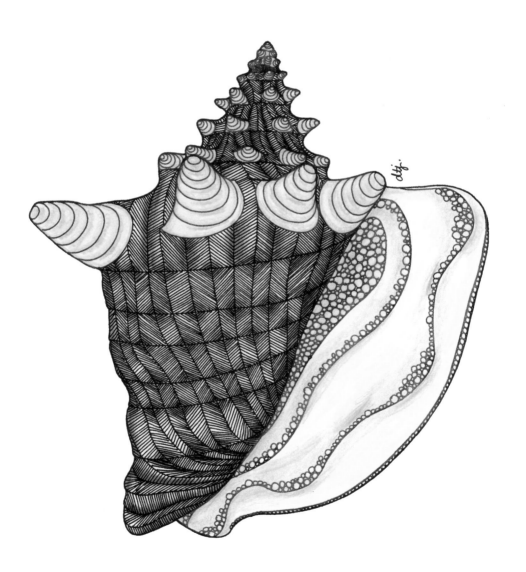

What is the best scent on Earth?

What is a class you would like to take?

What are you the best at?

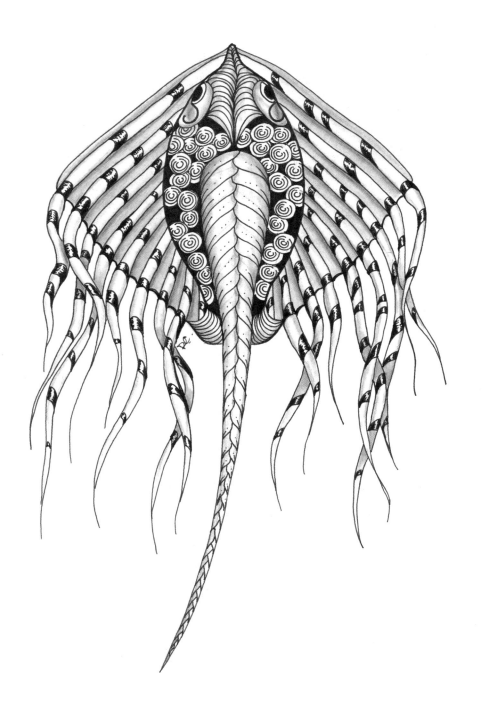

You just got a promotion! How do you celebrate?

What animal is most similar to you?

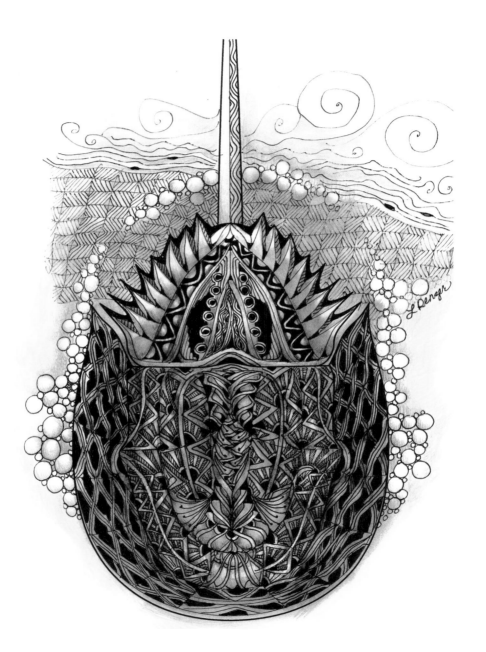

You can send your teenage self a letter with one piece of advice in it. What is it?

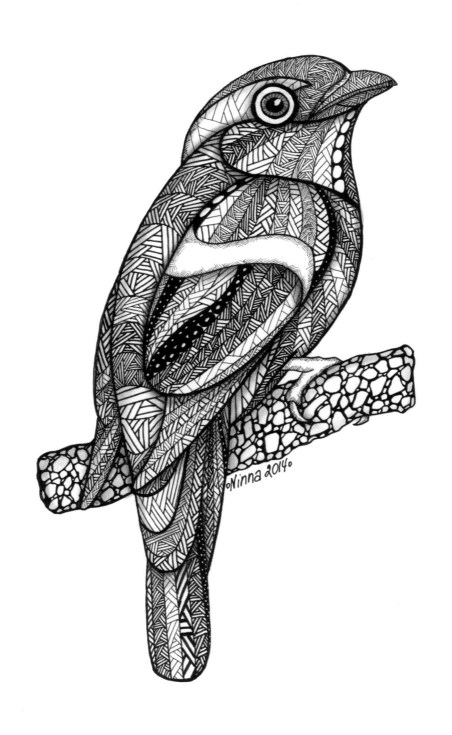
Ninna 2014

What's the best thing to do when you're at home during a thunderstorm?

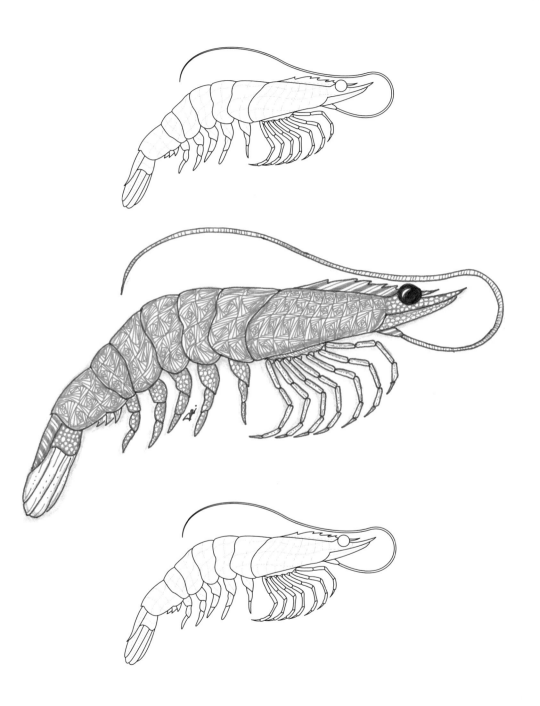

Set a goal for next month.
Set a goal for tomorrow.

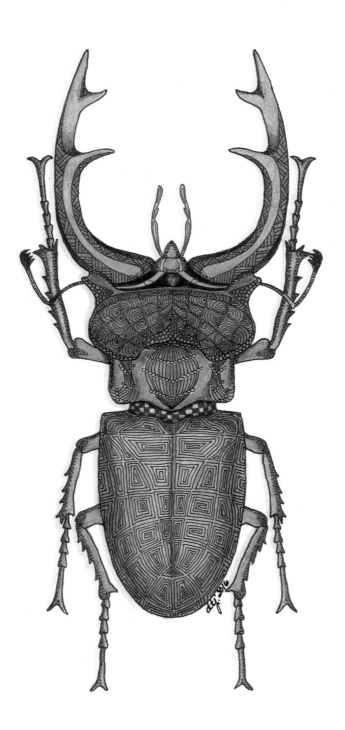

What makes you unique?

What is your earliest memory?

If you could have dinner with any three people, alive or dead, who would you choose?

Who is your biggest hero?

About the Artist

Ben Kwok (a.k.a. BioWorkZ) is an L.A.-based professional graphic artist. Working as an apparel designer, BioWorkZ has developed his own highly original hand-drawn illustration style. His distinctive illustrations evoke the popular Zentangle® drawing method and his client list includes Red Bull, Converse and Lucky Brand. Ben encourages you to join him in supporting animal charities such as the World Wildlife Fund. *www.WorldWildlife.org*

Other Craft & Drawing Titles from Ben Kwok

  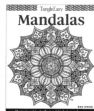  

Designs and Coloring by:

Cover – Marie Browning, CZT
Cindy Fahs, CZT
Chrissie Frampton
Candice Ferguson
Ninna Hellman
Darla Tjelmeland
Annie Jump
Elaine Sampson

Angela Carter
Abbey Gray
Diane Jennings
LeeAnn Denzer
Karen Grayczk
Marie Browning, CZT
Dawn Collins

ISBN 978-1-64178-008-7

Fox Chapel Publishing makes every effort to use environmentally friendly paper for printing.

© 2018 by Ben Kwok and Quiet Fox Designs, *www.QuietFoxDesigns.com*, an imprint of Fox Chapel Publishing, 800-457-9112, 903 Square Street, Mount Joy, PA 17552.

We are always looking for talented authors. To submit an idea, please send a brief inquiry to acquisitions@foxchapelpublishing.com.

Printed in China
First printing